THE FUNDAMENTALS
OF LIFE

THE FUNDAMENTALS
OF LIFE

ALLAN HOUSTON

IN PARTNERSHIP WITH THE ALLAN HOUSTON LEGACY FOUNDATION

The Allan Houston Legacy Foundation
260 West 39th Street
Suite 501
New York, NY 10018
www.AllanHouston.com

Published by
Mynd Matters Publishing
715 Peachtree Street NE
Suites 100 & 200
Atlanta, GA 30308
www.myndmatterspublishing.com

ISBN-13: 978-1-948145-25-1 (pbk) | 978-1-948145-26-8 (eBook)

FIRST EDITION

Printed in the United States of America

JOIN THE FISLL EXPERIENCE

Go to WWW.FISLL.LIVE for live events, webinars, rewards, and to download the FISLL app!

PREFACE

Everything started with a relationship. A particular relationship between a father and son spawned a chain of events that lasted an eternity. It began with the father spending an exhausting amount of time and energy creating a gift for his son.

When the time was right, he handed his son the gift and told him, "I have only made one of these, made to fit you perfectly and to last forever. Be careful how you use it because it has extreme power and will give you insight to all of my secrets and plans for you and our family."

The son opened the gift and found a pair of eyeglasses inside. It was like no other eyewear ever made. He told his son, "Now you will see from my eyes."

The son put on the glasses and immediately noticed that the father was looking in a large mirror. He asked him, "Why are you staring in the mirror?" The father replied, "Every day, I look at myself in this mirror. I wanted you to see that you are a reflection of me and I am a reflection of you."

At that moment, the son understood how much the glasses meant to the father. The son also realized how much *he* meant to the father. He knew he could not lose the glasses and needed to learn how to wear them responsibly. Wherever the son went, he took the glasses with him and they remained in perfect condition.

I studied the relationship between the father and son in more depth. I was amazed at how unique it was because it was different than a lot of the father-son relationships I had seen. As I reflected on the son's response to the father, I learned more about myself and began to think about my dreams and goals and who was there to help me reach them.

I started to see myself, the people around me, and the world from a better view. I learned my thoughts and ideas had life and my words were powerful. I learned my actions were long-lasting and my life was eternal.

Every relationship in life has a purpose.

Although some connections with certain people will be longer and deeper than others, each one has value because it teaches us how to judge and manage our interactions. The most important relationships are ones that bring trust, honesty, loyalty, selflessness, truthfulness, consistency, and satisfaction in seeing both people fulfill their destiny.

In an instance, words and actions can impact a life and through one encounter, we can change someone's life. Ultimately, one decision can alter our future.

**THINK ABOUT THIS:
WHAT WOULD YOU WANT PEOPLE TO
REMEMBER FROM THEIR EXPERIENCE
WITH YOU?**

When I asked myself this question, I realized I want people to live happier, more successful lives. I want to add value in someone's life so their future is brighter. I want to give them the five valuable principles I have learned along the way which are guaranteed to make their lives better.

CONTENTS

LIFE IS A GAME

"My only true opponent is the enemy
within me. He knocks at the door of my
thoughts but he won't enter. He whispers
at the cord of my soul but he won't be
heard. He stands in the path of my divine
calling but he won't misdirect me.
My victory is in the force of my focus,
the intensity of my preparation,
and the discipline of my execution."

WINNING

My sophomore year in high school was my breakout year as a scholar athlete. Our team lost the Kentucky State Championship in overtime to Clay County High School in Rupp Arena in front of 23,000 hard-core high school basketball fans. Very few of them wanted to see Ballard High School, from Louisville, win that game.

Playing for the University of Kentucky at that time was Rex Chapman, a basketball cult hero in the state of Kentucky and a future NBA player. After the game, he came into the locker room with some encouraging words, "Keep working. You have a chance to be really good!"

In Kentucky high school basketball, there are no classes according to school size or geographic location—one winner takes all.

The following year our team was determined to redeem ourselves. We faced the same team in the championship game and when the buzzer went off, we were victorious. I stood on the scorer's table facing the crowd, relishing the moment. I soaked in every second realizing it was something I'd never forget for the rest of my life, despite what I would achieve in the future.

We were all created for a purpose: to WIN.

We were designed to achieve and complete a divine assignment. Winning in life begins with desire. How great do you want to be? After desire is determined and communicated, expectation follows. How much do you believe you can achieve?

In life, we must train our mind and heart to think with those answers in mind and then put our body in position to function in a way that enables our desired outcome. If we don't, we will allow circumstances, and sometimes relationships, to defeat us and throw us off the path set for us. The only way we can guarantee success and keep the right perspective is being aware of the power of the spirit. The spirit gives us the energy, inner strength, and guidance to develop habits that will keep our mind and body functioning to WIN.

A healthy balance of the three dimensions of mind, body, and spirit is the key to being our absolute best and reaching our destiny.

"YOUR DESTINY IS YOUR CUSTOMIZED LIFE CALLING FOR WHICH YOU HAVE BEEN CREATED FOR MAXIMUM IMPACT."

TONY EVANS

We must be pushed and challenged to build this mindset and maintain this way of living. Our most important relationships will be with those that help us become better. Those who are holding us to higher standards. Those who are teaching us successful habits. Those who are teaching us to lead. Those who are helping us learn how to WIN in life.

We need to be put in a position to achieve what's possible, and we need to be able to receive this from someone we trust. Someone who is willing to be uncomfortable with us. Someone who can speak truth from a place of love and compassion.

The most dynamic leaders are receptive to truth and guidance. They realize they cannot be their best alone. We should all embrace their approach and search out those who will help us be accountable to being our best.

Within the *Fundamentals of Life,* we identify five essential principles that must be constantly reinforced. The fundamentals of Faith, Integrity, Sacrifice, Leadership, and Legacy provide a system of thinking and a playbook by which we can all WIN in life.

HOW DO YOU IMPACT WINNING?

Courtesy of the National Basketball Association

Every day I wake up and am reminded of this important question. One we must all answer for ourselves as we are participating in the game of life, and out to win. Throughout all of my years, I've never met someone who enjoys losing.

"SUCCESS IS PEACE OF MIND WHICH IS A DIRECT RESULT OF SELF-SATISFACTION IN KNOWING YOU DID YOUR BEST TO BECOME THE BEST YOU ARE CAPABLE OF BECOMING."

JOHN WOODEN

I often reflect on my youth, being raised by coaches, teachers, and community leaders. I think about how their teachings stuck with me and I am reminded of what tools I gained that have helped me learn the process of winning while never losing myself in the process.

Over time, I learned to compete against myself more than any opponent I faced. If I performed as well as I could, the results would be what they were supposed to be. The greatest performers I faced viewed winning as a habit of preparation and a mindset that had to be cultivated. It is a strategic way to approach competition and life.

Believe in the preparation, minimize mistakes, execute the plan, and put every ounce of energy into your craft. We keep the same attitude and spirit no matter the circumstances. Winning is not just the result of the score. It happens in the preparation and the learning as well as the competition. Over time, this becomes our mindset and our lifestyle.

REFLECTION:

What does winning in the game of life mean to you?

How does it apply to your life right now?

What winning habits do you want to create for yourself?

For more on Winning, download the FISLL app and join the conversation.

WINNING
IS A MINDSET.

LEADERSHIP
IS A LIFESTYLE.

IMPACT
IS ETERNAL.

WINNING
IS A MINDSET.

LEADERSHIP
IS A LIFESTYLE.

IMPACT
IS ETERNAL.

THE
BEGINNING

WE ARE ALL ON A JOURNEY. WE ALL HAD A BEGINNING.

All of our scripts are different, but they were written so those who believe would have victory in the end.

In 1973 Muhammad Ali returned home to Grand Avenue in Louisville, Kentucky after fighting Ken Norton. With his jaw wired shut, he stopped by our house to visit, which happened to be two doors down from his childhood home. It was also my second birthday. Whenever Ali would come back to Grand Avenue, he would bring a jolt of energy and positivity that made the street and neighborhood come alive. He never forgot his impact on people and culture as a whole.

My mother often reminds me and others that Grand Avenue has produced two gold medalists. To be able to say the greatest boxer and perhaps the most impactful athlete of all time and I have that in common is something I have always appreciated and never taken for granted.

Many may not know but I learned to walk on a basketball court. Literally, my first steps were ordered. I could say the game was destined for me. From my earliest memory, I've always loved to play

ALLAN AND ALI, 1973

basketball and I've always wanted to excel at anything I've done. When I was younger, games that involved any running didn't come easy for me because I needed corrective shoes and metal braces to support a deficiency that presented itself while I was developing.

Just a few years later, my parents were informed that I had a condition called Epiphysitis. The experts began to notice that the bones in my legs were growing apart and unbalanced in length. I don't remember much but when I think about it, I can still hear the clinging of the metal.

This state was my reality but it serves as a metaphor for all of our lives. Because life will present us with obstacles and challenges along the way, we need to be surrounded by people who will support and guide us. Having others hold us accountable so we stay on the right path provides a firm foundation to help us develop and reach our potential. Once we gain a better understanding of how to achieve our desires and win in life, we should want to pass that knowledge and insight to others so they can reach their potential as well.

We all have a divine assignment and a divine destination. The sooner we can embrace that truth, the sooner we will be on the path to functioning at our best.

REFLECTION:

What is something you've had to overcome?

Where did you find help?

How did this prepare you for where you are now?

Go to the FISLL app for bonus pictures, videos, and interviews with Allan.

THE
CHALLENGE

THE
CHALLENGE

I recently visited my old high school, Ballard High School, in Louisville, Kentucky. The current head coach asked me, "At what point in your life and career did you make your biggest strides in development?"

The first time was in high school when I was playing basketball against the best talent and competition available. I tried to find ways to match up and even though I felt pain in my knees from growing fast, my young body was getting strong enough and physically developing to the point where I could endure the challenge of playing against great college and professional players.

The second time was between my rookie and the end of my second season in the National Basketball Association. This time, I challenged myself more mentally to think at a higher level. I wanted to sharpen my focus and raise my expectations of what I could do with my talents.

The third point of my life and career where I experienced noticeable growth was immediately after I signed a free agent contract with the New York Knicks. It presented a different challenge that I accepted.

A conversation with my cousin also impacted me in a powerful way. He forced me to think even higher than I had been thinking. We spoke regularly after I relocated to New York and he was a source of clarity for me. He shared a scripture in the book of Proverbs that said, "As a man thinks in his heart, so is he."[1]

We discussed how the scripture translated to our lives. Since our actions follow the way we think about ourselves, we need to be in more control of that process. I view that moment as an opportunity to grow spiritually.

What I came to understand is that the highest level of thinking comes from our spiritual nature. The part of us that asks, "Why are we here?" and "What makes me special and unique from anyone else?" Or "What does God have planned for me?" and "What is He truly calling me to do?"

---

[1] Proverbs 23:7

I don't take those questions lightly and in fact, I took them so seriously that I began to try to answer them and apply them where I saw the need. I looked for people to inform and teach me. Almost immediately, I saw a difference in how I approached life. My renewed and clarified focus, in turn, increased my performance because I concentrated more on what was most important and prioritized my life and training better. I also had a clearer way to make decisions and better insight on who and what could help me reach the highest level possible.

As a competitor, we're always looking for a challenge. We need people to sharpen us when we're getting complacent and lazy. We need to be willing to be put in situations where we can be stretched so we can grow physically, mentally, and spiritually.

WE SHOULD ALWAYS CHALLENGE EACH OTHER TO LOOK HIGHER AND THINK DEEPER.

REFLECTION:

What has been your biggest challenge?

Who challenges you to be your best?

How do you challenge yourself to be better?

For more on The Challenge, download the FISLL app and join the conversation.

LIFE IN 3D:
MIND, BODY, SPIRIT

What does it mean to grow and get better physically, mentally, and spiritually? In order to see how we can reach our highest level, we need to understand how we were created and how we were made to develop as humans.

> **"WE ARE NOT HUMAN BEINGS HAVING A SPIRITUAL EXPERIENCE. WE ARE SPIRITUAL BEINGS HAVING A HUMAN EXPERIENCE."**
>
> PIERRE TEILHARD DE CHARDIN

What makes a human being special is that we are uniquely created. We were given incredible physical bodies with certain gifts, strengths, and talents that have the ability to think, believe in possibilities, and choose a path set for us. We were given the inner drive, heart, and motivation to connect to something bigger than ourselves.

This combination of intelligence, physical talent, and drive is known as mind, body, and spirit. All three dimensions of our being require special attention and each part of our being helps the others function.

Our body carries our physical activity and

genetic makeup. The body functions better with regulated and adequate sleep, breathing, exercise, diet, and other physiological needs.

Our mind holds our focus of attention, emotions, attitudes, behaviors, and choices. Our beliefs, positive thinking, mood, and resilience are all factors of the mind.

I believe the Spirit is the most important part of our being because it empowers us to see ourselves and act the way we were designed. It is our God-consciousness and where we find inner strength, direction, and guidance. It's where we receive our highest motivation, purpose, and meaning for life and reveals our ultimate desire to be connected to something bigger. It is our God-given life force that helps us think higher thoughts and gives us values and rules to live by.

Our overall quality of life and performance improves when we are led by our spirit. When we follow our spirit, it sets us on the right path. If I could use a prop to illustrate the three dimensions of mind, body, and spirit, I would use a smartphone. Even though we interface with the outer screen of the phone, we know it has an internal operating system. Inside each smartphone is a mobile technology that connects to other inner components of the device.

LIFE IN 3D

MIND

SPIRIT   BODY

SOURCE OF
Creative Energy
Internal Power   Physical Activities
Guiding Force   Nutrition, Sleep, Fitness
Passions & Desires
Purpose & Meaning

Thoughts, Choices, Emotions
Concentration, Focus, Stress, Mood

They allow the phone to function properly and execute the commands that we give with our fingers or voice. The outer body of the phone connects with the inner workings of the device. The inner workings are the brain and act as the mind of the phone.

It is commonly known that the most important function of the phone is to be able to connect with the outside world and to other people, which only happens through an invisible wireless signal. Without this signal, the smart phone is not functioning at its full capacity and it will be limited in its usefulness.

This is how the spiritual dimension works in us as humans. The spirit is the invisible force that connects our bodies and minds. It empowers us to communicate with our creator. Only through this divine connection can we be everything we were created to be. The spirit is the origin of the force that gives our mind and bodies the energy, power, motivation, and intuition to operate in abundance.

Our inner being (our mind) and outer being (our body) were designed to work together in a complex way, but without the connection to the source of unlimited power and data (the spirit), we cannot operate at full capacity.

The more we become aware of our inner being, the better we become at responding and processing things that happen throughout our lives. This inner consciousness contains our deeper thoughts and judgements that rest deep in our soul.

"THE MOST VALUABLE HUMAN POSSESSION IS OUR SOUL."

Our soul is our psychological and emotional center. It is like a non-material internal organ that catches our ideas, urges, attitudes, and behaviors. It manages our ability to choose and make decisions that affect our lives.

It is our true nature and personality that yearns to be in alignment with God and reflect His character.

GOD WANTS TO COMMUNICATE WITH US ON A PERSONAL LEVEL.

He wants to give us the secrets of success that He has laid out for us. If we expand our heart and mind, and listen to His voice, great things will happen for us.

The mission of three-dimensional (3D) life of mind, body, and spirit is to inform and equip people to be physically, emotionally, mentally, and spiritually fit and mature.

REFLECTION:

What does life in 3D mean to you?

How fit are you physically? Mentally? Spiritually?

How important would it be to focus on these areas in your life?

For more on Life in 3D, download the FISLL app and join the conversation.

ENERGY

The most intense series of games I've ever played were during the 1999 NBA Finals. Every possession became more important than the previous one. Every decision, every pass, every shot was critical. Because the stakes were so high and the competition so intense, I was physically, mentally, and emotionally drained after each game.

For the remainder of my career, recovery after the games became as important as preparation for them if I wanted to achieve maximum performance. I had to always keep balance in mind.

Life takes us through the same process. Each step forward takes an increased level of work and dedication. Every level we reach will require more time and recovery than the one before it to be our best.

Managing our energy could be the most valuable skill to learn. While we can't control how we're created, we can control the energy we put into being our best. The most important investment we can make is the proper investment in personal energy. We often put energy in activities and relationships that keep us on the wrong path instead of the right one. When we manage our energy properly, we give ourselves the best possible results.

"OUR MOST CRITICAL HUMAN RESOURCE IS ENERGY."

JIM LOEHR
Founder of Johnson & Johnson's Human Performance Institute

Energy is defined as the capacity to work. It is the fuel that makes things go. Think about the time and effort you put into something you're passionate about and want to excel in.

As human beings, where we place our energy determines our ability to develop, drives our performance, and helps us live healthier lives. If we want to maximize our potential, we have to make a serious investment.

"In each, energy can be systematically expanded and regularly renewed by establishing rituals—behaviors that are intentionally practiced and precisely scheduled, with the goal of making them unconscious and automatic as quickly as possible."[2]

If we can learn physical habits and behaviors like reading, eating, exercise, and muscle memory to create a pattern of movement with our bodies, we can create a desired pattern of habits with our attitude and thought process. We can increase our

---

[2] Harvard Business Review, 2007.

levels of motivation. This also takes discipline, but with practice, we have the power to increase our emotional control and focus when we think about and invest in our most meaningful values. We must continue to train to build a better way of life.

In the *Fundamentals of Life*, we will discover this pattern, the basic tools that keep the mind, body, and spirit in harmony, and the path to living a life of impact.

REFLECTION:

Why is energy important?
Where do you invest most of your energy?

For more on Energy, download the FISLL app and join the conversation.

LIFE

When my wife and I had our first child, I was overwhelmed with emotion. The night before she was born, we had just won the Eastern Conference Championship and were set to play the San Antonio Spurs in the 1999 NBA Finals. In one day, I went from playing in a playoff game to becoming a father playing for an NBA Championship.

Those twenty-four hours were as meaningful as any time in my life. In those moments, I didn't seem to have time to think about what kind of father I would be because I was completely focused on competing for the biggest achievement in sports. However, when I held my daughter, I could see and feel how fragile life was and I was overcome with gratitude as I recognized the true gift of life itself. In an instant, I felt both the joy of being a father and the joy of being a child of God.

> **"I HAVE COME THAT THEY MAY HAVE LIFE, AND THAT THEY MAY HAVE IT MORE ABUNDANTLY."**
>
> John 10:10 (NKJV)

We have been given the right to become children of God. We didn't choose our own physical birth, but we have been given a choice to give birth to a better life from within. This life goes beyond our physical capabilities. It is a new life where we begin to see from a better viewpoint. We are able to see past our obstacles and limitations. If you ever have been lost, injured, sick, felt hopeless or helpless, you realize how fragile we are as humans. We begin to accept that our days are numbered here on Earth.

At fifteen years old I made the most important decision of my life. I knew there was more than the here and now and when I heard a calling that spoke to my life, I knew it was God telling me to declare that I was going to choose the life He designed for me.

If we allow the Spirit of God to take over our heart and mind, we become more equipped to overcome anything that comes our way, and have the mindset to think above and beyond our expectations. In this way, we are more than conquerors. We aren't just participants in the game of life, we are winners. We are not just participants aimlessly walking through the seasons of life, we become game changers and impact players.

This is the abundant life. It is a peace of mind, knowing that God is in control and is working out every detail of our lives for our good if we trust Him. It is understanding that if we seek Him, despite our physical limitations, we will never lack the internal resources to build the life we desire.

Life is about looking at the big picture. It's maintaining an eternal perspective. As this becomes revealed to each one of us, we should want as many people as possible to experience that same lifestyle.

REFLECTION:

What kind of life do most people **want** to have?

What kind of life do **you** want to live?

For more on Life, download the FISLL app and join the conversation.

MOST PEOPLE
ULTIMATELY WANT:

To know their true purpose for living.

To be valued and validated.

To know their lives matter.

To know their lives have meaning.

To contribute something of importance.

A life of significance.

DEEP DOWN MOST PEOPLE WANT TO <u>CONNECT</u> AND <u>BELONG</u> TO SOMETHING <u>BIGGER</u> THAN THEMSELVES.

THE
FUNDAMENTALS

HOW DO WE KNOW WHEN WE ARE DOING THE THINGS NECESSARY TO BE OUR BEST?

To be successful in anything we need sound fundamentals. In basketball, for example, we recognize shooting, passing, ball handling, defense, rebounding, leadership, and awareness as key fundamentals that identify a well-rounded set of skills. Being proficient in these areas gives us the best chance for success.

We all are gifted with certain strengths. Fundamentals are the firm foundation that is laid beneath the gifts and talents with which we've been uniquely blessed. If we commit to building strong fundamentals, they will support and guide us in challenging and stressful situations. This is part of the evolution and growth needed to reach greatness. We can't run from them nor can we hide from them. If we have not committed to them, we will be weaker and fall apart when pressure comes.

We need a set of principles that gives us a foundation for impact and overall success.

FISLL RECOGNIZES 5 KEYS FOR SUCCESS:

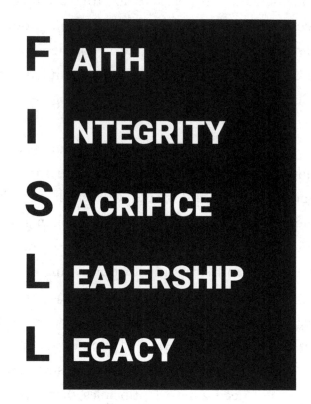

F AITH

I NTEGRITY

S ACRIFICE

L EADERSHIP

L EGACY

FAITH

BELIEVING IN YOURSELF,
YOUR PURPOSE, AND YOUR FUTURE

INTEGRITY

KNOWING THE RIGHT WAY
AND CHOOSING IT

SACRIFICE

COMMITTING TO
SOMETHING BIGGER THAN
SELF

LEADERSHIP

CAPACITY TO SERVE, MODEL,
INSPIRE, AND UNIFY

LEGACY

MAXIMIZING YOUR INFLUENCE AND
IMPACT

FAITH

FUNDAMENTAL ONE

WHAT DOES FAITH MEAN TO YOU?

Faith is expecting the most positive outcome. It is seeing beyond what's in front of you. It is believing in yourself, your future, and your destiny.

Benefits of a Focus on Faith:

- Evaluate your strengths and growth needs in order to make your uniqueness work for you

- Make your vision and aspirations clear and precise

- Exercise goal setting

- Determine your belief system

- Build confidence

- Develop trusting relationships

INTEGRITY

FUNDAMENTAL TWO

WHY IS INTEGRITY IMPORTANT?

Imagine a game with no rules or life with no boundaries. We need standards for right and wrong and good and bad to help us make better decisions, keep us on the right path, and live healthier lives.

Benefits of a Life of Integrity:

- Increased awareness of your moral compass

- Increased decision making skills

- Develop consistency in executing tasks

- Attention to detail

- Discovering the obedience factor

SACRIFICE

FUNDAMENTAL
THREE
_____

WHERE HAVE YOU SEEN SACRIFICE?

Sacrifice is making a commitment to something bigger than yourself. It's surrendering or putting aside your self satisfaction and comfort for something greater.

Benefits of a Life of Sacrifice:

- The art and power of surrender

- An understanding of service over self

- Increased level of discipline

- Expanded work capacity

- Heightened sense of self-control

LEADERSHIP

FUNDAMENTAL
FOUR

WHAT MAKES A LEADER?

Leadership is recognizing the greatness in others and helping them achieve it. It's the capacity to serve, model your own expectations, and inspire others to reach a higher level.

Benefits of Developing Leadership Skills:

- Deeper connections with others

- Learning servanthood

- Increased sense of responsibility

- Improved communication

- Understanding organization and management

LEGACY

FUNDAMENTAL FIVE

HOW DO YOU WANT TO BE KNOWN?

How will you maximize your influence and your long-term impact? Will you be known for making the world around you better?

Benefits of Building a Legacy:

- Understanding the power of your name

- Understanding the dynamics of mentoring

- Increasing your influence

- Discover your deepest motivations

- Seeing life from the highest perspective

REFLECTION:

What is something you like to do?

What is your occupation?

What is something you are good at?

What are the basic fundamentals that lead to success in that activity, sport, or job?

Which of the 5 fundamentals of life connect with you most?

For more on The Fundamentals, download the FISLL app and join the conversation.

COACH

In 1980, at nine years old, I watched my father's University of Louisville basketball team win the National Championship. Over the next seven seasons, Louisville made three more Final Four appearances, while winning their second National Championship in 1986. My father, Wade Houston, remained one of the top recruiters and assistant coaches in all of college basketball for thirteen seasons.

My father was widely respected and admired for his authenticity and ability to recognize greatness and potential. In 1989, he became the first Head Basketball coach at the University of Tennessee and the first African American head basketball coach in Southeastern Conference history.

I was asked recently, "As an All-American candidate and first team All-SEC for four seasons, how was it playing for your father as your coach at the University of Tennessee and how did it impact you, on and off the court?"

I thought of a lot of things but there is something my mentor once said that came to mind.

"EVERYONE NEEDS A COACH."

> **"A COACH IS ONE WHO TRIES TO GET THE VERY BEST OUT OF AN INDIVIDUAL. YOU'RE TRYING TO MOVE THEM FROM POINT A TO POINT B."**
>
> ALICE HOUSTON

What is the role and impact of a coach? In observing the best coaches I've played for and watched, FISLL has given me a framework and lens to answer this question.

Coaches are parents, guidance counselors, teachers, managers, pastors, facilitators, and advisors. A true coach not only teaches and trains a skillset to be prepared for advancement or competition, a true coach teaches life! They create a passion and hunger for life.

A coach is kerosene. There is an inner light in us that wants to become a flame. There is a light that strives to expose and eliminate darkness in human nature. The darkness in our hearts produces fear, doubt, selfishness, stubbornness, and narrow mindedness.

Darkness yields to light. A coach reveals those things in us that may limit us and they turn on our inner light or help make it shine brighter.

A good coach becomes the kerosene that sparks a flame in us—the spiritual capacity in us. Coaches inspire us to live better lives because they know if we live better, we perform better.

"ALWAYS BE THE HARDEST WORKER."

"EVERY DAY, YOU EITHER GET BETTER OR WORSE, BUT YOU NEVER STAY THE SAME. DETERMINE TO IMPROVE EVERY DAY."

WADE HOUSTON

REFLECTION:

What makes a good coach?

How important is a good coach in helping us learn about life?

What is a life lesson you've learned from a coach you've had?

What kind of coach would you be?

For more on being a great coach and/or being coached, download the FISLL app and join the conversation.

THE FISLL COACH

FAITH

- Proclaims a bold vision
- Gives confidence to the player, builds confidence in the player
- Identifies players' strengths and defines a success-driven role
- Establishes a high level of trust
- Sets aspirational but achievable goals

INTEGRITY

- Maintains high standards and consistency in word and deed
- Establishes clear team rules and boundaries
- Strategically teaches respect and character
- Teaches attention to detail
- Remains coachable

THE FISLL COACH

SACRIFICE

- Loves people
- Promotes selflessness (team before self)
- Teaches discipline & self-control
- Establishes strong work ethic & level of conditioning

LEADERSHIP

- Models their expectations
- Builds strong communication skills
- Fosters team
- Obtains 'buy-in' from individuals
- Teaches according to learning styles
- Empowers and teaches others to lead
- Maintains wisdom and discernment
- Manages relationships

THE FISLL COACH

LEGACY

- Is self-aware
- Understands the magnitude of their influence
- Prioritizes mentoring
- Provides a template & terminology to pass on
- Helps players see their purpose
- Maintains an "eternal perspective"

TRAINING

PURPOSEFUL AND PRACTICAL PREPARATION PRECEDES PROGRESS.

Success and maximum impact are intentional. They are not random and do not happen by accident, chance, or luck. They are the result of practice with consistency and precision.

Every choice we make influences the next moment and has a consequence, positive or negative. With each decision and action, we groove a pattern in our brain that produces a habit over time. This is a philosophy that applies in all areas of our lives. Whether it's our relationships, career, financial aspirations, or personal growth, we have the power to design the behaviors and levels of commitment that lead to success.

REFLECTION:

What kind of training are you participating in now?

What are you learning?

For more on Training, download the FISLL app and join the conversation.

IMPACT

EVERY SECOND,
EVERY MINUTE, MATTERS.

At Senator John McCain's memorial, former President, Barack Obama, referenced a quote in one of the senator's favorite books. "Today is only one day in all the days that will ever be. But what will happen in all the other days that ever come can depend on what you do today."[3]

In *Beginning*, I referred to moments that have the ability to change our lives. In an instant, a thought, an image, a word, or a conversation can impact us. I remember specific moments that were turning points in my life.

For the last fifteen years, I've also seen those moments occur in the lives of students, parents, teachers, coaches, and leaders all across the world when the *Fundamentals of Life* have been presented to them. I've seen the power of these principles at work as they produce self-awareness, resilience, and leadership.

Transformation means a change in nature or character. Through the *Fundamentals of Life*, I have seen a positive influence and a change in

---

[3] Hemingway, Ernest. For Whom the Bell Tolls Duty. Scribner, 21 October 1940.

perspective. If perspective enhances, one will have a better chance of making the adjustment in a positive direction. A shift in perspective and level of thinking and understanding come from something higher and deeper than our physical nature. It comes from more than just our physical or tangible experience. I can train my body to be in its best physical condition, but if the mind and soul are weak, I cannot be in the best condition possible.

God breathed life into us and that made us a living soul. His intention was not just to carry his image with our bodies, but with our personality. He has provided a way to fulfill his intention. We are being "transformed into his image with ever-increasing glory."[4]

In this belief, we find our purpose. We find encouragement in knowing our lives will have meaning and IMPACT. We find our highest motives and aspirations.

When we look to the principles of Faith, Integrity, Sacrifice, Leadership, and Legacy, we are challenged to then stand and live by them. Our purest and highest motive in life becomes bigger and higher than us. Why? Because it's all from Him.

---

[4] 2 Corinthians 3:18

Everything started with a relationship.

A relationship with a father.

REFLECTION:

Can you think of your most impactful moments?

How will we live our most impactful lives?

How can we be a positive influence on those around us to help them do the same?

For more on Impact, download the FISLL app and join the conversation.

The *Fundamentals of Life* show us how to have a positive and healthy view of ourselves. They give us a sound decision-making process and a personal code of behavior by which to operate. They force us to persevere through discomfort and adversity. They guide us as we guide others and have a strong positive influence. These five fundamentals have been given to serve as a framework for developing a winning mindset and successful habits.

REFLECTION:

What is your level of desire to win in life?

What is your level of positive expectations in your life?

What is your level of awareness in keeping high moral standards?

What is your level of willingness to surrender to a higher power greater than you?

What is your level of ability to lead others?

What is your level of awareness of your impact on others?

LIVE
BETTER.

PERFORM
BETTER.

LEAD
BETTER.

Visit www.FISLL.org to join the FISLL digital platform. Plus, get points, win prizes, and enjoy exclusive experiences. Launch your profile today!